CIVICS

Checks and Balances

By Cassie M. Lawton

Cavendish Square

New York

Published in 2021 by Cavendish Square Publishing, LLC
243 5th Avenue, Suite 136, New York, NY 10016

Copyright © 2021 by Cavendish Square Publishing, LLC

First Edition

Website: cavendishsq.com

This publication represents the opinions and views of the author based on his or her personal experience, knowledge, and
research. The information in this book serves as a general guide only. The author and publisher have used their best efforts in
preparing this book and disclaim liability rising directly or indirectly from the use and application of this book.

All websites were available and accurate when this book was sent to press.

Portions of this work were originally authored by Leslie Harper and published as *What Are Checks and Balances? (Civics Q&A)*.
All new material this edition authored by Cassie M. Lawton.

Cataloging-in-Publication Data

Names: Lawton, Cassie M.
Title: Checks and balances / Cassie M. Lawton.
Description: First edition. | New York : Cavendish Square, 2021. | Series: The inside guide: civics | Includes glossary and index.
Identifiers: ISBN 9781502656933 (pbk.) | ISBN 9781502656957 (library bound) | ISBN 9781502656940 (6 pack) | ISBN
9781502656964 (ebook)
Subjects: LCSH: Separation of powers–United States–Juvenile literature. | United States–Politics and government–Juvenile
literature.
Classification: LCC JK305.L39 2021 | DDC 320.473'04–dc23

Editor: Kristen Susienka
Copy Editor: Nathan Heidelberger
Designer: Tanya Dellaccio

The photographs in this book are used by permission and through the courtesy of: Cover Orhan Cam/Shutterstock.com; p. 4
Tanarch/Shutterstock.com; p. 6 Ken Wolter/Shutterstock.com; p. 7 JPL Designs/Shutterstock.com; p. 8 https://upload.wikimedia.
org/wikipedia/commons/9/9d/Scene_at_the_Signing_of_the_Constitution_of_the_United_States.jpg; p. 9 https://upload.
wikimedia.org/wikipedia/commons/6/6c/Constitution_of_the_United_States%2C_page_1.jpg; p. 10 Culture Club/Getty Images;
p. 12 Tom Williams/CQ Roll Call/Getty Images; p. 13 Marco Bello/Bloomberg via Getty Images; pp. 14, 20 Chip Somodevilla/
Getty Images; p. 15 chrisdorney/Shutterstock.com; p. 16 Andrey_Popov/Shutterstock.com; p. 18 MANNY CENETA/AFP via Getty
Images; pp. 19, 21 Carol M. Highsmith/Buyenlarge/Getty Images; p. 22 Patrick Semansky/AP Photo/Bloomberg via Getty
Images; p. 24 GEORGES GOBET/AFP via Getty Images; p. 26 STR/AFP via Getty Images; p. 27 Hill Street Studios/DigitalVision/
Getty Images; p. 28 (top left) Stock Montage/Getty Images; p. 28 (bottom left) Stefani Reynolds/Bloomberg via Getty
Images; p. 28 (right) https://upload.wikimedia.org/wikipedia/commons/e/e6/Andrew_Johnson_photo_portrait_head_and_
shoulders%2C_c1870-1880-Edit1.jpg; p. 29 (top left) J Main/Shutterstock.com; p. 29 (top right) Rawpixel.com/Shutterstock.com;
p. 29 (bottom left) Steven Frame/Shutterstock.com; p. 29 (bottom right) Joaquin Corbalan/EyeEm/Getty Images.

Some of the images in this book illustrate individuals who are models. The depictions do not imply actual situations or events.

CPSIA compliance information: Batch #CS20CSQ: For further information contact Cavendish Square Publishing LLC, New York, New York, at 1-877-980-4450.

Printed in the United States of America

Find us on

CONTENTS

Leaders of the legislative branch of US government, called Congress, meet in the US Capitol Building in Washington, DC.

UNDERSTANDING CHECKS AND BALANCES

Governments around the world have different leaders and laws, or rules. Each government works differently. Some governments give all the power to make decisions to one leader. Examples include absolute **monarchies** and dictatorships. These types of government can make life hard for people living in the country because one person makes all the decisions for everyone else. Other governments **distribute** power between many people. An example is a democracy, like the government in the United States.

Living in a democracy means the people who live there help make sure the government runs smoothly. They elect political leaders who help make decisions. They vote on important issues. They **protest** for changes when an issue is very important. Many people work together to make sure there's a balance of power in the government in a democracy.

Three Branches

An important feature of the US government is that it's divided into three branches, or parts. These branches are called the legislative branch, the executive branch, and the judicial branch. The three branches each have different roles, or jobs. Each branch works to make sure the other branches aren't too powerful. For example, the legislative and judicial branches help make sure the leader of the executive branch, called the US president, doesn't have too much power and follows the country's laws.

Marching to draw attention to issues is one way to hold government leaders accountable.

Checks and Balances

By separating different jobs and powers between the three branches, a system of **regulating** power is created. It's a system of checks and balances that makes sure one branch doesn't hold all the power. It was formed during the 1780s, after the United States broke away from Great Britain and became its own country. The **Founding Fathers** thought it was important to have the system in place to help the new country avoid becoming a monarchy, like Great Britain.

The checks and balances system is part of the US Constitution. This is the set of laws that set up how the country is run. The laws in the Constitution are some of the most important laws in the

legislative
makes laws

executive
carries out laws

Fast Fact

The different branches of US government include Congress (legislative), the president and vice president (executive), and the Supreme Court (judicial). They meet in Washington, DC, the US capital city.

judicial
interprets laws

These three branches form the US government.

THE US CONSTITUTION

The US Constitution is the highest law in the United States. It was written in the summer of 1787 in Philadelphia, Pennsylvania. The men who wrote it are often called the Framers. They set up a frame, or structure, for how the US government would work. Many of the Framers are also considered to be part of a group called the Founding Fathers because they helped start, or found, the country. Some of the most famous of the Framers were Benjamin Franklin, Alexander Hamilton, George Washington, and James Madison.

The Framers wanted power to be shared in their new country. To do this, they created the three branches of government. In the Constitution, the Framers created a way for all parts of the government to work together.

Fast Fact

The Constitution's different sections, called articles, describe the United States' different laws. They're written using Roman numerals, such as Article I or Article II.

The people who wrote the US Constitution met at what's now called the Constitutional Convention in 1787.

United States. They cover ideas like citizenship, voting rights, and basic freedoms. The US Constitution also defines the branches of government and their responsibilities.

According to the US Constitution, each branch can check, or limit, some of the powers of the other branches. This creates a balance of power in which no one person or group has too much control.

Shown here is part of the US Constitution, which set up the system of checks and balances.

Shown here is part of the US Constitution, which set up the system of checks and balances.

Fast Fact

If people don't like a law in the Constitution, they can try to change it. Any change made to the Constitution is called an amendment. There are 27 amendments today. The first 10 amendments are called the Bill of Rights.

The Fouding Fathers, shown here, didn't want one person to have control of the government.

THE BRANCHES OF GOVERNMENT

The three branches of government have been part of the United States since nearly the very beginning. They were developed when the country was just starting. Ever since, they have helped guide the country.

New Government, New Rules

After the United States declared independence from Great Britain in 1776, the country needed a government and people to lead it. In 1777, while the United States was still fighting for independence from Great Britain, the Founding Fathers adopted a set of laws called the Articles of Confederation. Instead of giving lots of power to a king, like in Great Britain, these laws allowed each individual state government to make most of its own decisions. The Articles of Confederation also gave powers to a national, or federal, legislature to make important decisions for the whole country, but these powers were very limited.

Soon, many people began to think the national government was too weak. It had trouble getting anything done. In 1787, the Framers wrote the US Constitution to replace the Articles of Confederation. The Constitution still allowed each state to have its own government, but it gave more power to the federal government. Because they were worried about giving any part of the federal government too much power, the Framers divided the

federal government into the three branches we have today and set up the system of checks and balances between those branches. The Constitution outlines these branches in its first three articles, or sections.

The US Congress meets to discuss important issues.

The Legislative Branch

The legislative branch is talked about in Article I of the Constitution. It's the part of the government that makes laws. It's made up of two groups: the Senate and the House of Representatives. The Senate is made up of 100 members, called senators. There are two senators for each state. The House of Representatives has 435 members as of early 2020. Its numbers are based on a state's population. If a state has a large population, it has more representatives than another state with a much smaller population.

Together, these two groups are called Congress. Members of the US Congress write laws and vote on which laws will take effect. They also have the power to collect money in the form of taxes, and they can vote to go to war with another country.

There's a balance between laws passed by the federal government and laws passed by the states. The federal government makes laws for everyone in the country, but states also make a lot of laws for people living in or visiting a state. Each state government has its own legislative branch. A state's legislature makes laws that apply only in that state.

The Executive Branch

The role of the executive branch is explained in Article II. Its job is to make sure that laws are executed, or carried out. The president leads the executive branch. They can approve or **veto** laws written by Congress and meet with the leaders of other countries. They also nominate people to serve on the Supreme Court and in other important positions.

President Donald Trump is shown here. Article II explains the president's job.

The vice president helps the president perform these duties. The executive branch also includes many departments concerned with issues such as education, energy, and housing. The heads of these departments are members of the president's **cabinet**. They meet with the president and give their advice.

The Judicial Branch

The judicial branch's responsibilities are defined in Article III. This part of the government is made up of the US court system. Its job is to interpret, or understand and explain, the laws of the country. The highest court in the United States is the Supreme Court. It's made up of eight judges, called justices, and a chief, or lead, justice.

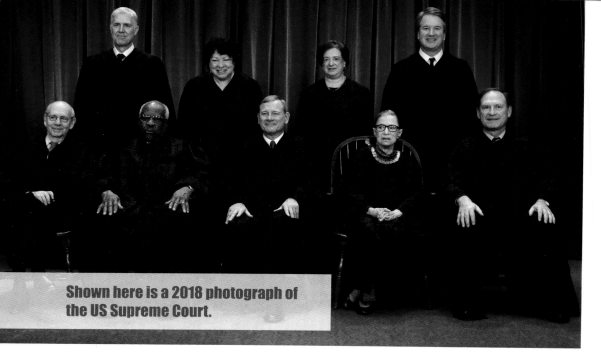

Shown here is a 2018 photograph of the US Supreme Court.

When a person or group feels that a lower court has made a mistake or that a law is **unconstitutional**, they can ask the Supreme Court to hear their case. The Supreme Court will listen to arguments and think about what a law means and whether it goes against the Constitution. The nine justices of the Supreme Court then make a decision by taking a vote. Their rulings on cases are decided by a majority. That means at least five justices must agree on a ruling.

Smaller courts around the country, called district courts and courts of appeal, also help make decisions about laws and citizens. They all form the federal judicial branch.

Fast Fact

At the front of the Supreme Court Building are carved the words "Equal Justice Under Law." The justices agree to make decisions for all equally, based on their understanding of the Constitution.

POLITICAL PARTIES

Within the United States, there are different groups, or parties, that political leaders belong to. The main political groups today are Democrats and Republicans. Each group has different values. Typically, Democrats are more liberal. They believe the federal government should play an active role in people's lives by helping provide health care and other social services. Republicans tend to be more conservative. They believe in limiting the power of the federal government and letting states and individuals make their own decisions about issues like health care and education.

Sometimes the party of the president is the same as the dominant party in Congress, and it's easy to create laws aligning with that party's beliefs. Other times, government control is split between the two parties, and conflicts arise. Both political parties must work together to get things done. On important issues, such as war or border control, the parties must work hard to find the best solutions.

Different animals are used to represent the two main political parties in the United States. A donkey represents Democrats, and an elephant represents Republicans.

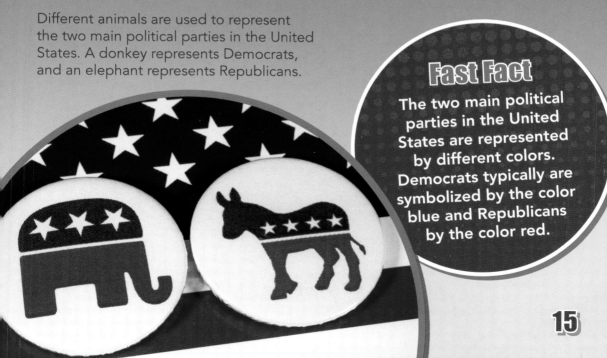

Fast Fact

The two main political parties in the United States are represented by different colors. Democrats typically are symbolized by the color blue and Republicans by the color red.

Like the scales of justice, the government's branches are meant to stay balanced.

LIMITING POWERS

The three branches of the government work individually and also together to ensure the system of checks and balances is carried out correctly. Checks and balances work like this: The executive and judicial branches limit the powers of the legislative branch. The legislative and judicial branches limit the powers of the executive branch. The legislative and executive branches limit the powers of the judicial branch.

Limiting the Legislative Branch

The power to write laws makes the legislative branch a very important part of the government. Laws are what make the government function. Members of the legislative branch, such as senators, can bring ideas for laws, called bills, before Congress. A bill goes through a series of steps before it becomes an official law. Sometimes, a bill never becomes a law.

The executive branch and the judicial branch limit the legislative branch's power, however. When Congress has voted to pass a new law, that law must be approved by the president, who's a member of the executive branch. The president can also choose to veto the law. Sometimes a person or group believes that one of Congress's laws is unconstitutional. People can ask the Supreme Court, the head of the judicial branch, to look at the law and decide whether or not it's unconstitutional. If it is, that law will no longer exist.

Bill Clinton, who's shown here, served as US president from 1993 to 2001.

Fast Fact

Three US presidents have been **impeached** as of 2020: Andrew Johnson, Bill Clinton, and Donald Trump.

Limiting the Executive Branch

Although the president leads the country, they can do little without working with the other two branches. The Senate, part of the legislative branch, must approve anyone whom the president nominates to serve on the Supreme Court or as the head of a cabinet department. The Senate must also approve formal agreements that the president makes with other countries. The legislative branch may impeach the president if they commit a crime or behave **corruptly** while in office. One of the president's most important jobs is leading the US military. This means the president has the power to command troops. However, only Congress can declare war.

Still, there are ways around these limits. A president can create directives or rules, called executive orders, for important issues. They can also order military attacks on other countries if there's an emergency. It's the responsibility of Congress and the judicial branch to ensure the president doesn't **abuse** these powers. For example, the Supreme Court can overturn an executive order if it's unconstitutional.

Fast Fact

If a president has vetoed a bill, Congress can still make it a law as long as two-thirds of each house vote to do so. This is called overriding a veto.

This is where the Supreme Court hears cases. The court can check the power of the legislative and executive branches.

Ruth Bader Ginsburg served on the Supreme Court through multiple battles with cancer before her death.

Limiting the Judicial Branch

Supreme Court justices serve until they either die or retire. The writers of the Constitution created the court this way so that, unlike the president and members of Congress, the justices could make hard decisions without having to worry about being elected or reelected.

The judicial branch is still limited by the other two branches, though. The president nominates people to become Supreme Court justices. The Senate must then approve those nominations. If a justice commits a serious crime, they can be impeached by a vote in Congress.

INTERPRETING THE CONSTITUTION

Different Supreme Court justices interpret the Constitution differently. Some justices are originalists. That means they think the words and intent, or purpose, of the Framers give the most pure understanding of the document. They look to the Framers' thoughts and viewpoints to decide if a law is constitutional. On the other hand, modernists examine the Constitution from a modern-day perspective. They wonder how it would be interpreted in today's world.

Another way of reading the Constitution is through literalism. There are two kinds of literalism: historical and **contemporary**. Both literalist approaches look only at the words of the Constitution. Historical literalists only consider the Constitution's original wording. This interpretation similar to originalism. A contemporary literalist, on the other hand, only follows the words of the Constitution but translates them into modern language, giving a more current reading of the text. For example, if the text reads "militia," a contemporary literalist substitutes that with "the National Guard" in today's terms. There's no single, correct way to interpret the document, and the different ways can create conflict and make decisions even tougher for the Supreme Court.

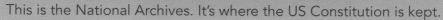

This is the National Archives. It's where the US Constitution is kept.

Members of Congress, like Nancy Pelosi, have important parts to play in balancing power in the US government.

BALANCING POWERS

The US government was created to make sure the balance of power is maintained. Every day, leaders of all the branches communicate with each other. Many of the people working for the government want the balance of power to be equal. They work hard to make sure that happens.

If a problem occurs, they talk about it and take action if needed. For example, in 2019, President Donald Trump was accused of abusing his presidential powers. The House of Representatives wanted to make sure he didn't become too powerful. They impeached him for abusing his power and for interfering with Congress's ability to oversee his actions.

Keeping the Balance

What do you think would happen if one person in the government held all the power? You likely wouldn't agree with all of that person's choices. The Founding Fathers worked hard to create a fair system of checks and balances. They wanted a government that would serve all citizens without allowing one person or group to become too strong.

Keeping this balance of power is one of the most important ways that our government stays fair. Our government works best when all three

Fast Fact

An important organization with a checks and balances system is the European Union (EU). As of 2020, it's made up of 27 different countries in Europe. They all work together to make decisions and distribute power among the nations.

The European Commission, the executive branch of EU government, meets here.

branches share power and work together. If one branch becomes too powerful, it's the responsibility of the other branches to work together to restore balance.

Sharing power between the three branches of government is not always easy. It's an important foundation of a fair government, though.

At Work Today

The system of checks and balances isn't only in the US government. Many other countries use a similar system, as do many local governments. State governments around the United States are modeled after the federal government and also have a checks and balances system. Even small organizations like schools and businesses can use this kind of system. Some schools might have committees that help maintain the balance of power in a school district. When groups work together, it can build a better world. More people can have opportunities to grow and become responsible citizens.

The Framers of the US Constitution wanted the government they created to become an example to many other countries around the world. Today, many nations look to the United States as a role model, or good example. Democracy is a popular form of government today because of places like the United States. Without a system of checks and balances, the United States and other countries like it could look very different.

Fast Fact

Many members of Congress have their own websites and their own social media accounts you can check out. Always ask a parent or guardian before going on any of these sites, however.

North Korea puts most of its power in the hands of a single leader, who's shown here. This can make life difficult for people in the country.

In a system of checks and balances, each person works to make sure their government runs fairly. However, this is not always the reality in the United States and other places that have this system. This is why it's important for leaders to step up if there are problems with one or more branches or if one person or branch is abusing their power. Leaders must carry out their duties as part of the system of checks and balances. It's also important that citizens elect people to office who will value the system of checks and balances.

Fast Fact

More than half the countries around the world are full or **partial** democracies.

WHAT CAN YOU DO?

It might seem like preserving checks and balances is the responsibility of people older than you. However, there are ways you can get involved too. One way is by writing letters to or calling your representatives in Congress to talk about topics you're passionate about. You can tell them your thoughts about an idea or event that's affecting the country. You can ask them to vote for or against a certain issue. You can also remind them of their responsibilities in the system of checks and balances. You can get in touch with representatives in your local or state government as well. Another method is to get an adult's permission to contact your representatives through social media. You can also get involved in community groups and help make sure the groups run smoothly. If there are problems, talk about them with other members. You too can help keep the government and society balanced.

People can help the government stay balanced by electing good decision-makers to Congress and other branches of government.

TIMELINE

A History of US Checks and Balances

1775–1783
The American Revolution is fought between Britain and America.

1777
The Articles of Confederation are agreed to by the Continental Congress.

1787
The US Constitution is written, and Articles I, II, and III outline the different branches of government.

1789
The first US Congress meets, and the US Bill of Rights is created.

1868
Andrew Johnson becomes the first president to be impeached.

1998
Bill Clinton becomes the second president to be impeached.

2019
Donald Trump becomes the third president to be impeached.

THINK ABOUT IT!

1. What are the three branches of government, and how do they work together?

2. What do you think about the checks and balances system? Would you have a system like it if you could create your own government?

3. How well do you think the system of checks and balances is working in the United States today?

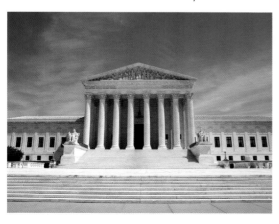

4. What actions can you take in your community to make sure different leaders don't become too powerful?

GLOSSARY

abuse: To hurt, damage, or overuse.

cabinet: A group of people who act as advisers to important government officials.

contemporary: Modern-day; present.

corrupt: Dishonest.

distribute: To give out or separate into smaller groups.

Founding Father: One of the men who helped form the United States and its government.

impeach: To charge someone in political office of misconduct. When someone is impeached, a trial is then held to determine if the person should be removed from office.

monarchy: A government that has a king or queen as its leader.

partial: Not complete.

protest: To join together publicly to demand change or action.

regulate: To manage.

unconstitutional: Going against the basic rules by which a country or a state is governed.

veto: To stop a bill from becoming a law.

FIND OUT MORE

Books

Bonwill, Ann. *We Have a Government.* New York, NY: Scholastic, 2019.

Demuth, Patricia Brennan. *What Is the Constitution?* New York, NY: Penguin Workshop, 2018.

Kowalski, Kathiann M. *Checks and Balances: A Look at the Powers of Government.* Minneapolis, MN: Lerner, 2012.

Websites

History: Three Branches of Government
www.history.com/topics/us-government/three-branches-of-government
This website gives an overview of the three branches and their history.

The US Government
www.usa.gov
Learn all about the US government by visiting the US government's official website.

White House: US Constitution
www.whitehouse.gov/about-the-white-house/the-constitution
The White House explores the history behind the US Constitution and lists the 10 amendments of the Bill of Rights.

Publisher's note to educators and parents: Our editors have carefully reviewed these websites to ensure that they are suitable for students. Many websites change frequently, however, and we cannot guarantee that a site's future contents will continue to meet our high standards of quality and educational value. Be advised that students should be closely supervised whenever they access the Internet.

INDEX